5/06

D0757676

Date Due

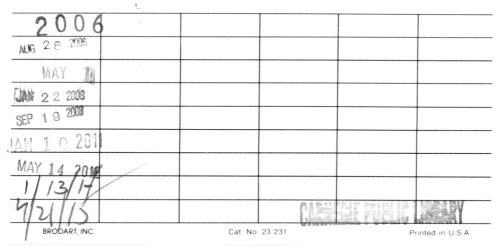

2006				
AUG 28 2006				
MAY 14				
JAN 22 2008				
SEP 19 2008				
JAN 1 0 2011				
MAY 14 2012				
1/13/14				
4/21/15			CARNEGIE PUBLIC LIBRARY	
BRODART, INC.		Cat. No. 23 231		Printed in U.S.A

DOGS SET IV

Boxers

Cari Meister
ABDO Publishing Company

visit us at
www.abdopub.com

Published by ABDO Publishing Company, 4940 Viking Drive, Suite 622, Edina,
Minnesota 55435. Copyright © 2001 by Abdo Consulting Group, Inc. International
copyrights reserved in all countries. No part of this book may be reproduced in any form
without written permission from the publisher.

Printed in the United States.

Cover Photo: Ron Kimball Studios
Interior Photos: Ron Kimball Studios (pages 5, 19), Corbis (pages 7, 9, 11, 13, 15, 21),
AP/Wideworld (page 17)

Editors: Bob Italia, Tamara L. Britton, Kate A. Furlong, Christine Fournier
Art Direction: Neil Klinepier

Library of Congress Cataloging-in-Publication Data

Meister, Cari.
    Boxers / Cari Meister.
        p.cm. -- (Dogs. Set IV)
    Includes bibliographic references (p.)
    ISBN 1-57765-477-3
    1. Boxer (Dog breed)--Juvenile literature. [1. Boxer (Dog breed) 2. Dogs. 3. Pets.] I.
Title.
        5-24-06
    SF429.B75 M38 2001
    636.73--dc21
                                                                    00-045383

Contents

The Dog Family

Thousands of years ago, humans trained wild dogs to be helpers and companions. Even today, some dogs look much like wolves. Dogs and wolves have many of the same **traits**.

Dogs and wolves both have excellent hearing. And their sense of smell is much better than a human's. They can track the scent of animals and humans over great distances.

Dogs and wolves belong to the same **family**, called Canidae. There are other members in the canid family, too. Jackals, dingoes, and foxes are all canids.

Today, there are more than 400 different breeds of dog. They were bred for many purposes. Boxers were bred to help humans work.

Like wolves, boxers will guard their territory.

Boxers

Boxers have been around since the late 1800s. They were bred from a mix of bulldogs and **mastiffs**.

Early on, butchers used boxers to help control cattle. People also used boxers in dogfights. Dogfights were outlawed. But that did not mean the end of the boxer.

Some people say boxers are named for the way they fight. Boxers stand up on their back legs and use their front paws to fight. They look like a human boxer fighting with fists.

Boxers were bred to be intelligent, strong, and fearless. They were one of the first dog breeds used in German police work.

Today, boxers help with search and rescue work. And some boxers serve blind people as guide dogs. They are also devoted family and show dogs.

Boxers can be trained to perform many tasks.

What They're Like

Boxers are smart and playful dogs with lots of energy. They love to play outdoors. Boxers are **muscular**. They can jump very high! Many boxers like to play with a Frisbee.

Boxers are alert and loyal. They can be good watchdogs. In the face of danger, boxers are very brave. They have great memories, too. This makes them great working dogs.

Some boxers tend to roam from their homes. Others may fight with dogs that they do not know. Boxers can be prevented from roaming or fighting. They just need plenty of exercise and **obedience training**.

Red Auerbach, former coach of the Boston Celtics, has a pet boxer.

Coat and Color

The boxer has a short, hard coat. Boxers do not need lots of brushing. But if you brush a boxer daily, its coat will be smooth and shiny. Plus, brushing **massages** a boxer's skin. Most boxers love to be brushed.

Boxers do not need to be bathed very often. Unless they roll in dirt or mud, boxers stay clean. And bathing a boxer too often can be bad for its skin.

Boxers can be **fawn**, **brindle**, black, or white. But fawn and brindle are the only colors recognized by the **American Kennel Club (AKC)**. Many boxers have white markings on their neck, chest, belly, and feet.

Black and white dogs cannot compete in some dog shows. But they can still be great family dogs. White boxers tend to have more health problems than colored boxers. Deafness is also common in white boxers.

White boxers sunburn easily.

Body Size and Shape

Boxers are medium-sized dogs. Male boxers weigh about 65-80 pounds (30-36 kg). They are about 23-25 inches (57-64 cm) tall from their shoulders.

Female boxers are a little bit smaller. Female boxers weigh about 50-65 pounds (23-30 kg). They are about 21-24 inches (53-60 cm) tall from their shoulders.

Boxers have square heads. They have blunt, broad **muzzles**. Some boxers have problems breathing because of the shape of their muzzles. Because of these problems, owners should not take boxers jogging.

Some people crop boxers' ears to prevent **infections** and **injuries**. This makes the ears stand up straight. Other people leave boxers' ears uncropped. This makes the dog's ears lay flat against its head.

A boxer's strong back legs help it to jump very high.

Care

Like all dogs, boxers need a yearly trip to the **veterinarian**. Veterinarians make sure dogs are healthy. They also give dogs shots to stop diseases.

Boxers have large eyes, but they hardly have any eyelashes. So their eyes are easily **infected**. If your dog's eyes have redness, take it to the veterinarian.

Boxers love to play with toys. They love to fetch. Boxers may like to chew on bones, but this can be dangerous. Some boxers will swallow bones whole. The bones can get lodged in their throats.

Boxers like lots of attention. They like to play with people or other animals. They won't play alone for very long.

An adult should walk a boxer on a leash at least once a day. Boxers are very strong dogs and could easily pull a child around.

Boxers love to play games
with their owners.

Feeding

Like all dogs, boxers like meat. Most dog foods have all the **nutrients** they need. Adult dogs only need one meal a day.

Boxer puppies need several meals a day. If you are going to get a puppy, check with the breeder. The breeder will tell you how much and how often to feed the puppy.

All boxers should have a special, quiet place to eat. Feed your boxer at the same time every day. Also make sure there is fresh water near your boxer's food. Do not bother a dog while he or she is eating. Let the dog rest after its meal.

Boxers can be sloppy eaters. Many boxer owners put a plastic mat under the food dish to make cleaning up easier.

Opposite page: Boxers need plenty of water after they exercise.

Things They Need

Boxers are great family dogs if they get the right care. With **obedience training**, boxers are well-behaved dogs. Without training, they may not obey. A boxer that does not obey will be hard to handle.

Boxers need to be around the people they love. Lonely boxers may chew on furniture or shoes. They might even roam away from home.

Boxers should be kept indoors. They cannot handle very hot or very cold weather. If you are walking a boxer in winter, put some **petroleum jelly** on the pads of his or her feet. This will protect the pads from the cold, hard ground.

Like all dogs, boxers need a dog **license** and dog tag. Then if your boxer roams away, people will know who to call.

Obedience training should start when boxers are puppies.

Puppies

A baby boxer will grow inside its mother for about nine weeks. When a boxer is about to give birth, she usually will not eat. She will begin to **pant** heavily. Her temperature will go down.

The mother needs a quiet place to have her puppies. Humans rarely have to help the boxer deliver her puppies. Boxers usually have eight or nine puppies at once!

The puppies are helpless at first. They do not open their eyes until they are about ten days old. But they grow fast! After eight to twelve weeks, the puppies are ready to go to their new homes.

Boxer puppies are very playful. But they also need plenty of rest. In fact, puppies need to sleep most of the day so that they can grow big and strong.

Boxer puppies need lots of attention.

Glossary

American Kennel Club (AKC): a club that studies, breeds, and exhibits purebred dogs.

brindle: a gray, tan, or tawny color with darker streaks or spots.

family: a group that scientists use to classify similar plants and animals. It ranks above a genus and below an order.

fawn: a light yellowish-brown color.

infection: a sickness in people and animals caused by contact with germs.

injury: harm or hurt to a body.

license: a tag worn by a dog to show that it has been registered with a city.

massage: to rub muscles and joints to increase blood flow.

mastiff: a breed of large, powerful, smooth-coated dogs often used as guard dogs.

muscular: having many well-defined muscles.

muzzle: the jaws and nose of an animal; snout.

nutrients: important parts of a diet that all living things need to survive.

obedience training: teaching a dog or other animal to listen to your commands and obey.

pant: to breathe heavily.

petroleum jelly: an odorless, tasteless gel used to moisturize the skin.

trait: a feature of an animal.

veterinarian: a person with medical training who cares for animals.

Internet Sites

Boxer World
http://www.boxerworld.com
On this site, you can leave a message on the message board, chat in a chat room, and more! Look at the funny boxer pictures and read poems celebrating this breed.

Discovery Channel's Guide to Dogs
http://animal.discovery.com/dog_guide/dog_guide.html
Learn some fascinating facts about dogs on this site from Animal Planet. Learn which breed of dog would be best for you, and how to take better care of your dogs.

How to Love Your Dog
http://www.howtoloveyourdog.com
Here's a site just for kids. Learn how to be your dog's best friend. Read stories, test your knowledge of dogs, and read some doggy riddles.

These sites are subject to change. Go to your favorite search engine and type in boxers for more sites.

Index